A Guide to the National Anthem

God Save the King

Introduction by Anne-Marie Minhall

Illustrated by ROSIE BROOKS

First published in Great Britain in 2023 by Hodder & Stoughton
An Hachette UK company

1

Introduction Copyright © Anne-Marie Minhall, 2023
The right of Anne-Marie Minhall to be identified as the Author of the Work has been asserted by
her in accordance with the Copyright, Designs and Patents Act 1988.

Illustrations Copyright © Rosie Brooks, 2023
The right of Rosie Brooks to be identified as the illustrator of the Work has been asserted by
her in accordance with the Copyright, Designs and Patents Act 1988.

The words of the National Anthem – Public Domain

A CIP catalogue record for this title is available from the British Library

ISBN 978 1 399 80991 7

Printed and bound in Italy by L.E.G.O. S.p.A.

Hodder & Stoughton policy is to use papers that are natural, renewable and recyclable products and made from wood grown in sustainable forests.
The logging and manufacturing processes are expected to conform to the environmental regulations of the country of origin.

Hodder & Stoughton Ltd
Carmelite House
50 Victoria Embankment
London EC4Y 0DZ

Introduction

The story behind *God Save the King* is
an extraordinary one. Its foundation
is one of the oldest prayers we know. It
was first recorded in the Bible as it was
prayed over King David more than
3000 years ago, in around 1010 BC.

Since then, it has been prayed at the
coronation of every British monarch since
King Edgar the Peaceful, in Bath in AD 973.
But *God Save the King* has moved from a
spoken prayer to a national declaration,
and proud part of our identity.

In 1745 as King George II's reign was threatened by Prince Charles Edward Stuart, also known as Bonnie Prince Charlie, the musicians at the Theatre Royal in Drury Lane took the song as their own. One evening the band leader ended a performance with *God Save the King*. According to one newspaper report, there was 'universal applause from the audience' and then the music and words spread to the other playhouses in London, too.

Each night, the theatres would ring out with the sound of this anthem being sung by performers and audiences alike. Soon the horizons broadened, and *God Save the King* was being heard around the country.

Within a year or so it was being played and sung whenever royalty appeared in public.

'All the way upon the road we rarely proceeded five miles without encountering a band of the most horrid fiddlers, scraping God Save the King with all their might, out of tune, out of time and all in the rain . . .'

The English satirical novelist Fanny Burney describes a visit with the Court to Cheltenham in the late 1700s.

Around a century later the National Anthem as we recognise it today began to take shape. Although the words have been changed many times over the centuries, there are still officially five verses – but only one or two are ever really used in our times.

The monarch who messed around with it most was the music lover Queen Victoria. As the first sovereign to regard it as 'the national anthem', she enjoyed adding extra verses to celebrate births and marriages in the royal family.

In the twenty-first century at royal and military events, the National Anthem has to be played in a specific way – it's even written out in the King's Regulations for the Army:

'The first bars will be played pianissimo at M.M. 60 crotchets, using the full reeds, horns and basses . . . (the brass will be brought smartly into playing position on the third beat of the fifth bar) . . .'

And from the traditional to the contemporary, our National Anthem was the first song to be played by a computer; the musical notes of *God Save the King* were programmed by Alan Turing in the Computing Machine Laboratory at The University of Manchester in 1951.

Whenever and however this musical treasure is played it is instantly recognisable.

It plays a huge part in all our lives from childhood onwards. We all recognise those unique national occasions when the United Kingdom comes together and we share that anthem, that moment in history. It is deeply woven into our lives. Those times are never forgotten.

To celebrate 50 years of the reign of Queen Elizabeth II, rock star Sir Brian May stood on the roof of Buckingham Palace (brave!) and played the National Anthem on his electric guitar – broadcast live to millions of people around the world.

'Forever I will be proud of that moment because that was really breaking barriers, breaking frontiers. And so much could have gone wrong. I'm so grateful that it didn't!'

Sir Brian May

And 10 years later, the anthem broke new barriers when London hosted the Olympic Games in 2012. In the magnificent opening ceremony, the National Anthem was performed by deaf and hearing children in sign language.

But it's the times when people join forces and sing the iconic words that can really send a shiver down your spine. When that familiar, much-loved patriotic song echoes around sports stadiums and concert halls anywhere in the world; when we hear school choirs and orchestras play it with unbridled joy, and when those celebrations then become part of our spontaneous renditions! The heart can swell.

> *'Nothing tugs at the heart strings harder than a national anthem being belted out in a packed stadium by emotional athletes and thousands of their supporters.'*
>
> Ian Reid, CEO at Birmingham 2022

Beethoven was a fan. He once even declared that it was the best National Anthem that he had ever encountered – praise indeed!

'I must show the English . . .' Beethoven wrote, *'what a blessing they have in* God Save the King.*'*

The German composer reinvented the anthem for the piano as well as intertwining the theme into another creation, Beethoven's *Wellington's Victory.*

Our National Anthem is such an iconic piece of music that touches all our lives.

Timeless. Enduring. Evergreen.

May it always be this way. An anthem that is a constant in good times and in hard times.

Long live our noble King!

God save the King!

Send *him* victorious,

 *Happy and glorious,*

Long to reign over us,

God save the King.

Thy choicest gifts in store,

On him be pleased to pour,

Long may he reign.

May he defend our laws,

And ever give
us cause,

To sing with

heart and voice,

God save the King.

P.S. William IV listened to an odd performance of the anthem when he and Queen Adelaide opened the new London Bridge in 1831. They dined in the middle of the structure and, during the meal, a man and a woman walked forward:

'He was playing God Save the King *with his knuckles on his chin, accompanied by his wife's voice. I told [the King] I was sorry they had intruded without permission. "Oh, no. No intrusion" said the King. "It was charming. Tell them to perform it again."'*